All THINGS FROGS & TOADS For Kids

FILLED WITH PLENTY OF FACTS, PHOTOS, AND FUN TO LEARN ALL ABOUT FROGS & TOADS

ANIMAL READS

WWW.ANIMALREADS.COM

THIS BOOK BELONGS TO...

_____

_____

WWW.ANIMALREADS.COM

WHAT'S THAT CROAKING IN HERE?

Welcome to the Pond! 1

What Are Frogs and Toads? 5

Frog and Toad Superpowers! 17
   Characteristics

Amazing Species of Frogs & Toads 33
   of the World

Bouncy Homes 55
   Where Do Frogs & Toads Live?

What Do Frogs and Toads Eat? 65

Ribbit, Croak, Squeaks, and Screams! 75

From Tiny Egg to Jumping Frog 81
   The Life Cycle of Frogs and Toads

A Frog-tastic Farewell 89

Thank You! 93

WELCOME TO THE POND!

How would you like to meet some of the earth's coolest, slimiest, and **croakiest** super-jumpers?

Welcome to the fascinating world of frogs and toads, where the next unbelievably cool fact is just one *ribbit* away.

Frogs and toads are extraordinary animals. Not everyone appreciates them, but everyone should! Not only do they keep pesky insects at bay, but they are also part of a very exclusive animal crew. In this group, every member can live in two different environments, as if by magic.

Oh, you didn't know that frogs and toads begin their lives completely underwater, just like fish when they're young, and only hop on land when they grow up?

Well, prepare to be amazed because there are so many more cool facts about frogs and toads to discover in this book. Like the fact that frogs and toads can breathe through their skin. Isn't that just *the coolest thing ever*?!

Frogs and toads are outstanding creatures; we bet they are stoked that **YOU** want to learn about them. As you flip through these pages, you will learn everything that makes these animals so unique. You'll discover where frogs and toads live and what they love to munch on, the different species that exist, and all the impressive superpowers that make them stand out in the animal world.

Ready to leap right into the world of frogs and toads?

ALL THINGS FROGS & TOADS FOR KIDS

Let's go!

TIME **TO CROAK UP**

S**O**ME **FUN!**

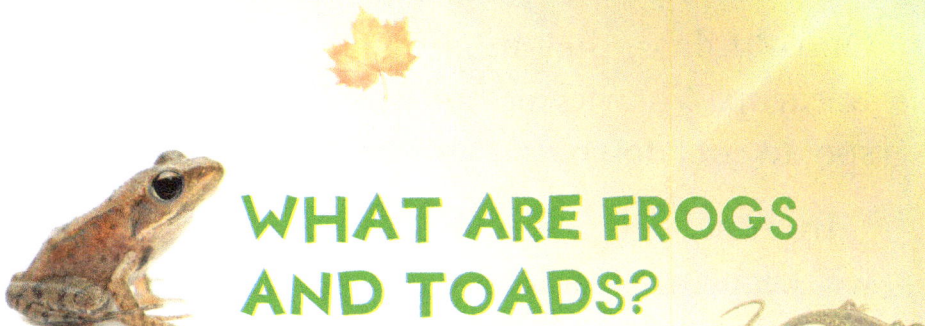

WHAT ARE FROGS AND TOADS?

Frogs and toads are special animals called **amphibians** (am-FIB-ee-ans). What makes amphibians so cool? They have three amazing superpowers!

First, they start their lives in water and then can live on land when they grow up. Second, they have special skin that can soak up water and even help them breathe! And third, they are **ectothermic** (ek-toe-THUR-mik), which means their bodies change temperature based on their surroundings. Even though that was a challenging word, this last trait is pretty neat!

Ectothermic means "cold-blooded," but it's not what you might think! It doesn't mean their blood is actually cold. It means that animals like frogs, toads, snakes, and turtles can't make their own body heat like we can. Instead, they need to find warm or cool places to keep their temperature just right.

On cold days, they might sit in the sunshine to warm up. When it's too hot, they'll find a nice, shady spot to cool down.

By now, you might be wondering, "Why do we keep using different names, aren't frogs and toads *the same animal*?!"

Here's a fun fact that scientists agree on: **toads are actually a type of frog!** All toads belong to the frog family, but they have some unique features

Just soaking up some warmth... frog style!

that make them different from other frogs. It's like how squares are a type of rectangle, but not all rectangles are squares.

This is a green toad... and the face it makes when it realizes it's actually a frog!

One of the main differences between typical frogs and toads is their preferred **habitat** (HAB-i-tat), which is a fancy way of saying "where they live."

Most frogs live near water and wetlands, while toads can live in drier areas like fields and grasslands. This is why they have different skin, and this is by far the easiest way to tell them apart! Frogs usually have smooth, moist skin that helps them stay cool and hydrated. On the other hand, toads have bumpy, dry skin that allows them to live in drier places and spend more time on land.

FROG vs TOAD

Frogs also have longer legs, so they are fantastic jumpers! Toads have shorter legs, which makes them great hoppers. **Frogs leap, and toads hop!** Another fun difference is that frogs often have bright skin colors, like green or red, which helps them blend in with the leafy or swampy surroundings they love. Toads usually have more earthy colors, like brown or gray, to help them match rocks, dirt, or grass.

ALL THINGS FROGS & TOADS FOR KIDS

The more you learn about them, the more you'll notice what makes each special!

I'd say we're all pretty special!

Fun Fact to Remember:

All Toads Are Frogs, But Not All Frogs Are Toads!

Think about it this way: frogs are like a big family, and toads are a special group within that family. They're like cousins who share some family traits but also have their own "toady" unique features. Isn't that neat?

Anywho... where were we?

Amphibians, right? THANK YOU!

EXAMPLE AMPHIBIANS

Axolotls

Frogs

Salamanders

So, frogs and toads belong to the amphibian family, which also includes salamanders and axolotls (AX-oh-lot-uls)... that's a mouthful to say! Within this amphibian family, frogs and toads are part of a group called "**Anura**" (an-OOR-ah). This word comes from Greek and means "without a tail." And it's true, grown-up frogs don't have tails at all!

Super fun fact:

Frogs are born with tails, but then they lose them!

Frogs and toads start life as tiny eggs floating in water. They then grow into wiggly little tadpoles with tails. After a little while, they sprout legs and say goodbye to their tails until, finally, one day, they hop right out of the water and onto land as grown-ups. This amazing process of change, called **metamorphosis** *(met-uh-MOR-fuh-sis), is one of nature's most magical transformations.*

A tail might help with balance... but luckily, I have other tricks up my sleeve!

WHY DO SCIENTISTS CREATE ANIMAL CLASSIFICATIONS?

Imagine walking into a library filled to the brim with books, and you're looking for a particular comic book. Typically, you would rely on librarians to *categorize* books by topic and section, right? Otherwise, how would you know where to find your comic book if a comics section didn't exist?!

Scientists do the same thing with animals, creating "classifications" in the animal world like librarians create "sections" in libraries. They group

animals with similar traits, looking at how they look, where they live, what they eat, and even how they are born.

By classifying animals, scientists can better understand what makes frogs different from fish or birds, and how all these animals are connected to each other. It helps them organize all the millions of different animals on Earth, just like organizing books makes a library useful!

A tiny toad balancing perfectly on a finger!

WHAT HAPPENED TO THE FROG THAT PARKED IN THE WRONG ZONE?

His car was TOAD!

FROG AND TOAD SUPERPOWERS!
CHARACTERISTICS

Earlier, we learned that frogs tend to be quite colorful, while toads' skin colors are more earthy and neutral. The coolest part of all of this is that some frogs have the amazing ability to **change color**, something they do when they need to hide from hungry predators. The ability to blend into the surroundings is called **camouflage** (KAM-uh-flahj), and it's an absolute lifesaver. Think of it like having a super cool invisibility cloak that changes color whenever you need to disappear!

Let's learn more about the incredible body parts of frogs & toads.

LEGS

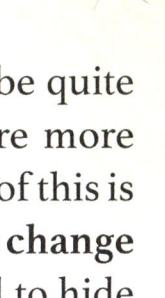

Frogs have super strong, springy legs that allow them to jump high and far. A frog can leap 10 to 20 times its body length! Imagine if you could jump like that... you could jump over your house or even

across a basketball court in a single bound. These powerful legs also help frogs catch their dinner, like tasty insects that might be flying or crawling nearby. *Maybe it's lucky you don't have to jump over your house just to catch your dinner!*

On the other hand, toads don't hop too far at all, maybe only one to three feet (30–90 cm) at most. So, while a frog can "outrun" a predator, a toad cannot "out-hop" a predator and relies more on camouflage to stay safe.

*Do you remember what **camouflage** means? It's when an animal's color or pattern helps it blend in with its surroundings, making it hard to see!*

ALL THINGS FROGS & TOADS FOR KIDS   19

SKIN

The skin of frogs would have to be one of its *bestest* features. Although they have lungs and can breathe through their noses and mouths, frogs and toads also use their skin to absorb oxygen. This allows them to stay alive, even underwater or in damp places.

If you've ever touched a frog, you **might have noticed that their skin feels a little slimy**. That's because frogs have a layer of oily **mucus on their skin** that protects them from bacteria **and other germs** and helps them stay moist.

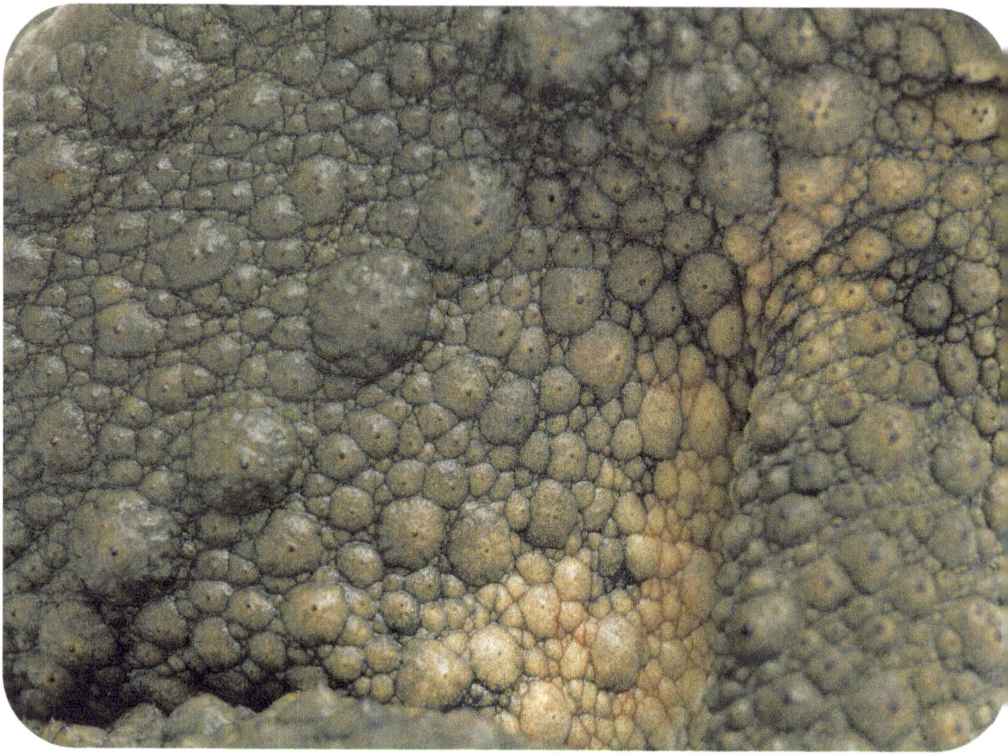

A close-up look at the bumpy skin of a giant river toad!

On the other hand, toads have drier and bumpier skin that doesn't feel nearly as slimy when you touch them. Their rougher skin helps them live in drier habitats, where they don't need to stay as moist as their frog cousins.

EYES

Frogs and toads have large, bulging eyes that sit high on their heads, which allows them to see al-

most all the way around without moving an inch. This helps them spot insects for dinner and predators lurking nearby. If you've ever tried to catch a frog or toad, you know they're hard to sneak up on, right? They can see you sneaking up on them, even if it seems they're looking the other way!

Another cool thing about frog and toad eyes is that they can push their eyeballs down into their head to help them swallow food. When they close their eyes and push them downward, it helps push food from their mouth down their throat.

Those big eyes don't miss a thing... I see you!

Fun Fact:

Frogs and Toads Can See in the Dark!

Frogs and toads have large eyes specially adapted to see in low light. This gives them the ability to hunt bugs at night and avoid predators who might be lurking

around in the dark. Imagine being able to see perfectly in the dark, that would be an awesome superpower to have, right?

HEARING

Many people think frogs and toads don't have ears because they are hard to spot. They certainly have ears, although they look very different from ours! Frogs and toads have eardrums on the outside of their heads that help them detect sounds from far away. They have excellent hearing, which allows them to find a mate, listen out for danger, and communicate with other frogs.

MAGICAL TONGUES

Now, let's talk about one of the things that frogs and toads are most famous for... their long, sticky tongues! If you've ever watched a frog or toad eat, you'll know that their tongues are incredibly fast.

When a frog or toad sees something tasty, like a fly or a beetle, it can flick its tongue out, stick to the prey, and pull it back into its mouth, all in the blink of an eye.

We bet you can't lick an ice cream as fast as a frog can stick out its tongue!

What makes a frog's tongue so special? For starters, it's attached to the front of its mouth instead of the back, like ours. This allows the tongue to shoot out straight and fast, giving the frog or toad a better chance of catching its prey.

Their tongues are also covered in a thick, gooey saliva that can change how sticky it is. When the tongue hits the prey, the saliva becomes super sticky, so the insect can't escape. Then, when the tongue pulls back into the mouth, the saliva changes again, becoming less sticky so the frog or toad can easily swallow its snack.

How's that for a superpower?!

A frog's tongue is soft and stretchy, almost like a rubber band. This stretchiness helps the tongue wrap around the prey, making sure it doesn't get away. Did you know a frog's tongue can stretch to

about one-third of its body length? Some frog species can even shoot out their tongues in just 0.07 seconds, that's 5 times faster than you can blink!

Frogs and toads rely on this marvelous tongue to catch all sorts of insects, which is excellent news for us because it helps keep the pesky bug population under control. *Thank you, frogs and toads!*

THE GREAT WINTER SNOOZE OF FROGS AND TOADS (HIBERNATION)

Have you ever seen a frog or toad wearing a cozy sweater or a warm coat? Probably not! But since frogs and toads don't have fur or feathers to keep them warm, they go looking for a cozy place to sleep for the winter as soon as the temperatures drop. This long winter snooze is called **hibernation** (high-bur-NAY-shun).

Some frogs sleep in the mud at the bottom of ponds, where the water stays warmer than the air

A cozy hibernation burrow!

This little guy just woke up from his long winter sleep!

above. Even though the water might be very cold, it doesn't freeze completely at the bottom, keeping the frogs safe. Other frogs and most toads dig little burrows in the ground, curling up in the dirt to stay safe from the cold.

During hibernation, their body systems slow way down, so they don't need to eat or move much. They sleep through the winter, waiting for warmer weather to wake them up in the spring. It's like taking one super long nap!

Fun Fact:

Other Animals That Hibernate.

Frogs and toads aren't the only animals that hibernate. Bears, groundhogs, and even some kinds of ladybugs take long naps during the winter, too. Hibernation helps animals survive when food is scarce and the weather is too cold for them to be active. Imagine just sleeping all winter long!

HOW DOES A TOAD FEEL WHEN HE HAS A BROKEN LEG?

Un-HOPPY!

AMAZING SPECIES OF FROGS & TOADS
OF THE WORLD

The world is home to over 7,000 different species of frogs, 500 of which are species of toads. These hoppy little creatures are among the most diverse animal groups on Earth! Frogs and toads live on every continent except Antarctica, where it is far too cold for them (and us) to survive in the wild.

Frogs come in all shapes and sizes, from the tiniest thumb-sized critter to some as big as a dinner plate! Some are epic masters of camouflage, blending in with leaves or rocks, while others stand out with bright, bold colors that scream, "Don't you dare mess with me!"

Let's meet some of the coolest frogs and toads!

AMERICAN BULLFROG

The American bullfrog is one of North America's largest and most impressive frogs. These giant, bouncy amphibians can grow up to eight inches (20 cm) long, as big as a small melon! Bullfrogs are known for their deep, booming call that sounds a lot like a cow's moo, which is how they got their name.

If you've ever been near a pond or lake on a warm summer evening, you might have heard the bullfrog's loud "jug-o-rum" sound echoing across the water. It's their way of telling other frogs, "This is

my pond!" Only male bullfrogs make this sound, using special pouches called **vocal sacs** (VOH-kul saks) that inflate like balloons when they call.

Fun Fact:

Bullfrog Super Eaters.

*Bullfrogs can swallow prey that's as big as their heads! They can gulp down surprisingly large meals thanks to their stretchy mouths and stomachs. A bullfrog could even eat a creature as big as a small **bird**, mouse, or another frog in one gulp! Scientists call bullfrogs "opportunistic predators" because they'll eat almost anything they can fit in their mouths.*

POISON DART FROGS

Poison dart frogs are tiny, colorful frogs found in the rainforests of Central and South America. Although small, most species are only about 1 to 2 inches (2.5 to 5 cm) long, about the size of your thumb, these frogs pack a powerful punch. They come in bright colors, like electric blue, sunny yellow, or flaming red, a tactic to warn other animals to stay away.

Poison dart frogs have a **toxin**, or poison, in their skin that can be very dangerous to predators and even to humans. Some rainforest tribes use the poison from these frogs on the tips of their blow darts for hunting, which is how the frogs got their name. But don't worry: these indigenous people don't harm the frogs to use their toxin. They only have to **rub the dart on the frog's skin** while being very careful not to touch them with their bare hands. Rubbing the dart on the skin is enough to transfer the poison, how cool!

Did you know that poison dart frogs aren't born poisonous? They develop their toxins from the special

insects they eat in the wild. Poison dart frogs raised in zoos eating different foods aren't poisonous at all!

There are over 100 poison dart frog species, each with its unique color pattern. The golden poison dart frog is one of the most toxic animals on earth, a single frog contains enough poison to affect up to 20 adult humans! But don't worry; poison dart frogs only use their toxins for defense, not for hunting, and they'll leave you alone if you leave them alone.

Fun Fact:

Nature's Warning Colors.

Many animals use bright colors to warn predators that they're dangerous or poisonous. This is called **"aposematic coloration"** (ap-oh-seh-MAT-ik). In this way, the poison dart frogs' bold colors are a message to potential predators, "Stay back, I'm poisonous!" It's like a flashing neon sign that warns of danger! Isn't it polite of nature to warn of danger?

I'm just here to warn you with my bright colors!

TREE FROGS

As their name suggests, tree frogs love to hang out in trees, climbing and jumping from branch to branch. They are found all over the world, from tropical rainforests to backyards in your own neighborhood. Tree frogs come in many sizes, from tiny ones less than an inch long to giants like the White-lipped Tree Frog of Australia that can grow up to 5.5 inches (14 cm) long!

While they may not make the longest jumps, tree frogs are famous for making the highest jumps of all. Some tree frogs can jump more than 7 feet (2 meters) straight up into the air! That would be

like you jumping as high as a two-story building in a single leap!

Tree frogs are particularly cunning, changing color to match their surroundings and blend in with tree bark or leaves. Many have bright-colored eyes that can startle potential predators when they suddenly open them. This surprise tactic gives the frog precious extra seconds to escape!

Tree frogs also have some of the loudest calls of all frogs. They use their elastic vocal sacs to create thunderous noises you wouldn't believe are coming from such a small animal! On a quiet night, some tree frogs can be heard from up to a mile away!

Study me closely and learn the art of climbing!

Fun Fact:

Frog Grip.

Tree frogs have unique toe pads that help them stick to almost any surface. These toe pads contain tiny, sticky cells that act like suction cups, allowing tree frogs to climb straight up smooth glass or cling to slippery leaves, even in the rain. They are so special that scientists are even studying them to create new sticky tools that might help people climb better.

NORTHERN LEOPARD FROG

The Northern leopard frog is named after its beautiful, spotted pattern that looks just like a leopard's coat. These medium-sized frogs grow to about 2 to

 ALL THINGS FROGS & TOADS FOR KIDS   43

4.5 inches (5 to 11 cm) long and can be found in ponds, marshes, and slow-moving streams across North America. They're excellent jumpers with smooth, greenish-brown skin covered in dark spots.

Leopard frogs are not what we'd call picky eaters, they gulp up a variety of insects, spiders, and even small animals, like smaller frogs or fish. Yikes! They are **opportunistic predators**, which means that if any foodie opportunity comes past them, they snap them right up!

Fun Fact:

Leap Like a Leopard Frog.

Northern leopard frogs are known for their powerful legs, which help them leap great distances. They also use these strong legs to escape predators quickly. They can leap up to 15 times their body length in a single bound! If you could jump like a Northern leopard frog, you could jump over four cars parked in a row. That would be a cool party trick!

BUDGETT'S FROG

The Budgett's frog, native to the wetlands of South America, is a unique frog that looks a bit like a cartoon character. These medium-sized

frogs can grow up to 3 to 4.5 inches (8 to 11 cm) long. They have round, flat bodies, and broad, smirking mouths, making them look hilarious. Their quirky looks have earned them funny nicknames, like "hippo frog."

Despite their hilarious and friendly appearance, Budgett's frogs are rather aggressive **ambush predators**, which means they hide and wait for their prey to come close. When an unsuspecting insect or small animal approaches, the frog lunges forward with all its might and captures it with its large, sticky tongue. We guess one must be a big eater to have such a big belly!

Fun Fact:

Growls and Screams.

Unlike most frogs, Budgett's frogs don't just croak or ribbit. When they feel threatened, they emit a sharp, high-pitched scream that sounds like a baby crying out for lunch! This strange call can surprise predators and startle humans!

AMERICAN TOAD

The American toad is one of the most common toads in North America, and you might have seen one hopping around your neighborhood! These medium-sized toads typically grow to about 2 to

You can't see me... or can you?

4 inches (5 to 10 cm) long. They are usually brown, reddish, or gray and love to hide in moist, dark places during the day. They look for food in the evening, hopping around and munching on bugs like beetles, worms, and spiders. With their earthy colors and bumpy skin, American toads are masters of camouflage. They can blend so well with fallen leaves and rocks that they're almost invisible to the untrained eye.

Fun Fact:

Look how BIG I am!

American toads don't rely solely on hiding for protection. They have special glands behind their eyes that release a bitter-tasting toxin. This defense keeps most predators from turning them into a snack! Some toads also puff up to look larger, making themselves seem more formidable than they are. Thanks to their defensive skills, American toads can live up to 10 years in the wild.

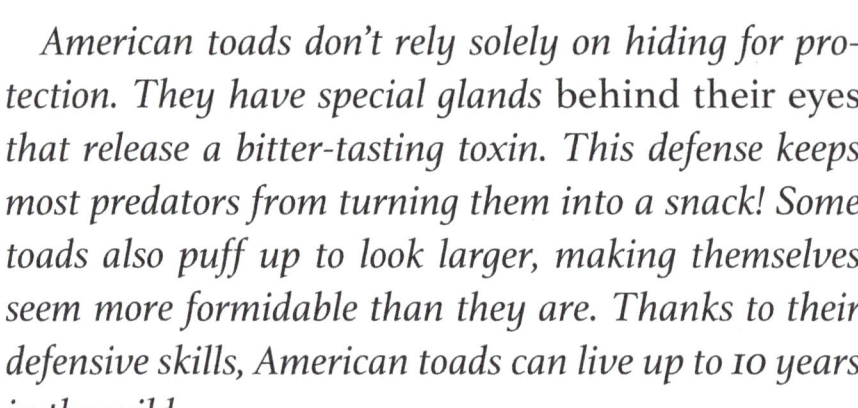

CANE TOAD

The cane toad is a giant among toads, growing up to nine inches (23 cm) long and weighing a whop-

ping three pounds (1.9 kg)! Originally from Central and South America, cane toads were introduced to places like Australia to help control pests. However, they quickly became pests themselves, causing problems for local wildlife.

When a cane toad feels threatened, it releases a strong toxin from glands on its back. This toxin is so powerful that it can harm or even kill animals that try to eat it. Because of their large size and high toxin levels, cane toads don't have to worry much about predators. They spend their nights hunting insects like beetles and ants; their large appetites mean they eat a lot! In places where cane toads have

spread, they've even helped reduce the number of mosquitoes and other pests, but they've also had harmful effects on local wildlife.

Fun Fact:

Egg-Laying Champions.

Cane toads are incredible when it comes to laying eggs. A female can lay up to 35,000 eggs in just a single year! While not all eggs will hatch into tadpoles and survive, those that do grow into big, hardy toads.

FIRE-BELLIED TOAD

One of the most colorful members of the toad family, the fire-bellied toad is known for its bright

colors and unique warning signals. These tiny toads grow to about two inches (5 cm) in length, making them relatively easy to spot. These toads communicate with each other by making soft, purring sounds and prefer to live in wet, swampy areas across Asia and Europe.

While the back of this toad is usually either green or black, their belly is where the magic happens. Bright red and orange stripes cover their bellies, a bold warning to any would-be predators. When danger is near, the fire-bellied toad flips over to show off its bright red belly, *and do you remember what this says in the animal word?* That's right, this speedy move is like flashing a red stop sign, telling predators to back off!

ANIMAL READS

Did you know?

Some birds of prey have learned how to hunt and safely eat poisonous frogs using several smart tactics. While some will only eat the legs (which usually have lower levels of poison), others pick up the frog and rub it on a tree trunk to remove the poison from its skin before eating it. How incredible is the circle of life in nature?

BOUNCY HOMES
WHERE DO FROGS & TOADS LIVE?

Frogs and toads are some of the most adaptable creatures on the planet. They can survive almost anywhere, from rainforests to mountains and deserts to suburban backyards. Keep an eye out the next time you're outside, especially after a rain. You might spot a froggy friend nearby, just waiting to hop into action!

Here are some of the places where frogs and toads are commonly found:

TROPICAL RAINFORESTS

Some frogs and toads enjoy the warm and humid climates of **tropical rainforests**, places where it rains a lot and stays warm all year round. Rainforests provide plenty of food, water, and hiding places where frogs can stay safe from predators.

One of the most famous rainforest frogs is the red-eyed tree frog, which climbs trees and clings

to leaves with sticky toe pads. It's an expert at blending in with green leaves during the day and comes out at night to hunt for insects.

Although toads are mostly known to enjoy drier areas, several species, like the Crested Forest Toad, love the humidity and nutrition of a rainforest too!

DESERTS

Believe it or not, some frogs also live in **deserts, where they** have amazing adaptations to survive

in the dry, hot conditions. Desert-dwelling frogs, like the Australian Water-Holding Frog, have special waterproof skin that helps them conserve water. They dig deep holes in the sand, where they can hide from the harsh heat and stay cool.

These desert frogs are incredibly patient, they might stay buried for months or even years, waiting for rain! When it finally rains, they quickly emerge from their burrows, splashing happily in temporary puddles and frantically catching insects and finding mates before the water disappears again.

Jaw-dropping fact:

Desert frogs can hide and sleep for YEARS!

Some species of desert frogs, like the Spadefoot Toad and Water-Holding Toad, can sleep in deep burrows for up to 7 years if the desert has a super dry spell between big rains!

This is a Sonoran Desert Toad! It only comes out at night and burrows underground during dry periods.

WETLANDS

If you were to imagine an ideal habitat for frogs and toads, it would have to be **wetlands,** like marshes

Ahh, the wetlands... my favorite place to be!

and swamps. For animals that need both water and land, wetlands are perfect. The shallow water provides a safe place for frogs to lay their eggs, and tadpoles have plenty of room to swim and grow. The mix of water plants, mud, and land areas creates lots of hiding spots and hunting grounds.

Some of the most common wetland frogs include the Green Frog, Chorus Frog, and Spring Peeper. Their calls create a beautiful nighttime symphony in spring and summer!

Frozen but fearless... ice, ice, froggy!

COLD REGIONS

Despite them seeming to be tropical animals, some species of frogs have also adapted to live in **colder regions**, even in forests where the ground is covered in snow for months. The Wood Frog, which lives as far north as the Arctic Circle, has a remarkable superpower, **it can actually freeze solid during winter!**

Up to 65% of the frog's body water turns to ice, and its heart completely stops beating. Special chem-

icals in its blood act like antifreeze, protecting its cells from damage. When spring arrives, the frog's body thaws out, its heart starts beating again, and it hops away as if nothing happened! This amazing adaptation allows these frogs to survive in places where other frogs couldn't live.

Fun Fact:

Toads Are Better Adapted to City-Life!

No matter the season, this little wood frog can handle it!

While frogs and toads share similar habitats in nature, toads are often better at adapting to human environments. They love to live in fields, grasslands, and even towns and cities! Although their skin is drier than a frog's, it can actually hold even more water, so they can live in much drier places, like your suburban backyard where most frogs couldn't survive for very long unless you built them a pond!

You can spot me in cities, backyards, and maybe even on your school campus!

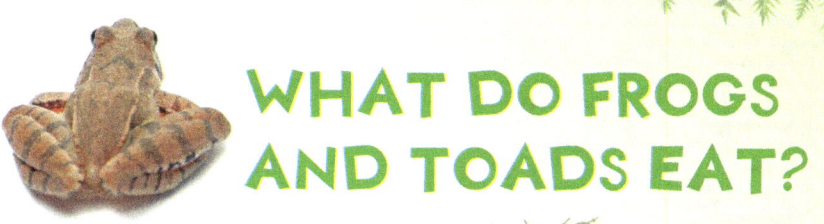

WHAT DO FROGS AND TOADS EAT?

Frogs and toads are **carnivores** (KAR-ni-vors), meaning they love eating meat... though you don't need to worry that they'll hop up to steal your hamburger. They don't eat *that* kind of meat! Instead, they are mostly **insectivores** (in-SEK-ti-vors), meaning their favorite meal is insects.

As you can imagine, the smaller the frog, the smaller the meal. Tiny frogs and toads might stick to a menu of tiny insects like flies, mosquitoes, and beetles. They catch their meals with their lightning-fast tongues, which can shoot out and back in less than a second!

Larger frogs and toads, however, can tackle much bigger prey. Along with bugs, they might eat worms, slugs, snails, and sometimes even small fish. A few **bigger** frog species, like the American Bullfrog, are **even** known to eat other frogs, small reptiles, and occasionally small mammals like mice! For these **hungry** hunters, just about anything that fits into their wide mouths is fair game.

Frogs and toads don't chew their food the way we do. Instead, they swallow it whole! Once they've caught a bug or other small prey, they push it down with their tongues and let their stomachs break it down. They sometimes use their eyes to help push food down, they close their eyes and pull them down into their head, which moves the food toward their throat!

Fun Fact:

Bug Busters.

A single frog can eat more than 100 insects in one night! By munching on so many mosquitoes, flies, and

other bugs, frogs help keep the insect population under control. This makes them nature's fantastic pest controllers! Farmers sometimes even use frogs instead of pesticides to protect their crops from insects.

PREDATORS

Despite their clever camouflage, super quick reflexes, and sometimes toxic skin, frogs still have several predators they must watch out for. Many animals consider frogs and toads a tasty snack! Their small size and abundance make them an easy target for various hunters, though we have learned that frogs and toads have developed a range of defenses to try and keep themselves safe.

Watch out, frogs! This heron is on the hunt!

Birds are some of the biggest threats to frogs and toads. Herons, kingfishers, and other water-loving birds swoop with sharp beaks to snatch these amphibians from the water's edge. Owls and hawks also hunt for frogs in forests and grasslands, using their keen eyesight to spot them even when they're hiding.

But frogs and toads don't only have to watch out for flying predators. On the ground, creatures like raccoons, foxes, and even otters find them delicious.

Frogs and toads that live near water are especially at risk, as these animals can easily spot them when they come up to the surface. Even domestic pets, like dogs and cats, are known to chase and sometimes catch frogs and toads.

Reptiles, especially snakes, are also major predators of frogs and toads. Snakes are incredibly good at being super sneaky, striking quickly before the frog has a chance to hop away. Even larger and slower reptiles, like turtles, may snap up frogs if they get close enough.

Other **water creatures** also pose a threat. Large fish, like bass and pike, can gulp down frogs in a single bite. Water bugs and diving beetles might even eat tadpoles before they have a chance to grow into frogs!

Fun Fact:

Defense Modes.

*Let's sum up all we have learned about the defense mechanism of frogs... Some rely on **camouflage** to protect themselves, while others have even more dramatic defenses. Toads, for instance, can **puff themselves***

up to look larger and **release toxins** from glands in their skin that taste bad to predators. Poisonous frogs, on the other hand, use their **bright colors** to warn predators not to come too close. And, of course, some frogs and toads use their incredible **jumping abilities** to escape, leaping away from danger in a flash.

Shhh... just making sure no predators can find me!

ANIMAL READS

This African Bullfrog is puffing up to look BIG and tough... and it's working!

Warning: I'm poisonous! Predators, stay back!

WHAT DID THE FROG SAY ABOUT HIS FAVORITE BOOK?

Reddit, reddit, reddit!

 # RIBBIT, CROAK, SQUEAKS, AND SCREAMS!

Have you ever sat outside on a summer night and heard the chorus of frogs and toads filling the air? Sure, it may seem like they're just making noise, but every sound you hear has a particular meaning, like a secret frog language!

ROMANTIC SERENADES

One of the most common reasons frogs make sounds is to **attract a partner**, so consider it a froggy serenade. Male frogs and toads are the ones who do most of the calling, singing loud and proud to let the females know they're ready to start a family.

Each frog species has its own unique call, so even among a mixed community of frogs, females know precisely which call belongs to the males of their same species. Isn't that amazing? These love songs can range from deep croaks to whistles or chirps.

DANGER ALERTS

Frogs also have special calls to **warn each other of danger.** When a frog spots a predator, it can make a sharp, high-pitched scream or a series of short, sharp croaks. This alarming noise not only startles the would-be predator but also alerts other frogs and toads nearby, giving them a chance to escape.

The American Bullfrog even makes a unique high-pitched squeak when it's scared or grabbed.

WEATHER FORECASTERS

Some frogs even have a special "**rain call.**" Before a storm, certain frogs get excited and start

calling more than usual, almost as if they're predicting or announcing the upcoming rain. People have noticed that frog calls often increase just before it rains, making frogs excellent "predictors" of weather!

Scientists think frogs can sense changes in air pressure and humidity that happen before rain. When these conditions are just right for laying eggs, the frogs get excited and start calling.

Everybody, RUN! Or... I mean, HOP!

TERRITORY DEFENDERS

And like all animals, frogs and toads appreciate their **personal space.** When a frog claims a particular territory, it lets out a territorial call to warn others to stay away. This is especially common during mating season when male frogs compete for the best spots near water where females are likely to gather.

By calling loudly, each frog is saying, *"This is my space, find your own!"* Sometimes, male frogs even have wrestling matches to defend their territory, pushing and shoving each other with their front legs until one gives up and hops away!

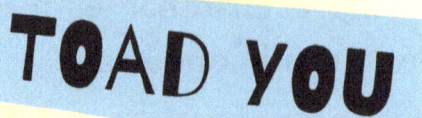

TOAD YOU IT'D BE FUN!

FROM TINY EGG TO JUMPING FROG
THE LIFE CYCLE OF FROGS AND TOADS

Frogs and toads have one of the most exciting life cycles in the animal world, changing from tiny eggs in water to leaping adults on land.

Female frogs and toads lay eggs in water, usually in large clumps or long strings. These eggs are

This common brown frog is guarding her eggs!

usually protected by a thick, jelly-like coating that keeps them safe from bacteria, predators, and other dangers.

Frogs typically lay their eggs in calm, shallow water, where there's little risk of the eggs being washed away. Some species lay hundreds or even thousands of eggs at a time, increasing the chances that at least *some* of them will survive.

TADPOLES

After a few days or weeks, the eggs hatch into tadpoles. Tadpoles look more like tiny fish than frogs

They may look like tiny fish, but they're actually tadpoles!

at this stage, with round bodies, long tails for swimming, and gills for breathing underwater. They don't have any legs yet!

For the first few weeks, a tadpole's main job is only to eat and grow strong. Unlike adult frogs that eat insects, tadpoles mostly munch on algae and tiny plants in the water. They're like mini underwater vegetarians, building strength and preparing for the big changes ahead.

METAMORPHOSIS

As tadpoles grow, they go through an amazing transformation called **metamorphosis** (met-uh-

These tadpoles have sprouted legs, and their eyes are moving up... soon they'll be little frogs!

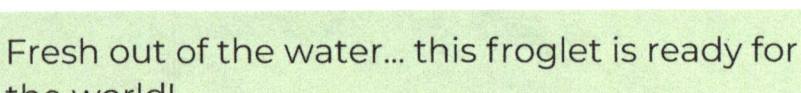

Fresh out of the water... this froglet is ready for the world!

MOR-fuh-sis). First, tiny back legs begin to sprout. Then, weeks later, the front legs appear. At the same time, their tails begin to shrink, and lungs slowly develop to replace their gills.

During this time, their digestive system changes too, getting ready to switch from a plant diet to an insect diet. Their mouths widen, and their tongues develop. Their eyes even change position, moving higher on their heads!

ALL THINGS FROGS & TOADS FOR KIDS

Depending on the species, this stage can take weeks, months, or even a year. Almost every organ in their body changes during this transformation to prepare them for life on land. They become "froglets" or "toadlets," basically mini versions of adult frogs and toads.

ADULTS

Finally, the tadpole's tail disappears completely, and it becomes a fully grown frog or toad. With solid legs for hopping, lungs for breathing air, and

A young toad enjoying a flowery throne!

a sticky tongue for catching food, it's ready to leave the water and explore life on land.

Once fully grown, these frogs and toads may eventually return to the water to lay their eggs, starting the life cycle again.

Fun Fact:

Life Cycle Champions.

While most frogs and toads complete their transformation in a few weeks, some species take much longer. For example, the bullfrog can stay in its tadpole stage for up to two years! This extended childhood allows bullfrogs to grow larger before they transform into adults. On the other end of the scale, some desert-dwelling frogs can speed through metamorphosis in just 8-9 days when they need to, racing to become adults before their temporary rain puddles dry up!

A FROG-TASTIC FAREWELL

Well, haven't we hopped through quite an adventure together? From exploring the lush rainforests where tree frogs dwell to diving into the cool, murky ponds of toads, we've journeyed across the globe and back. Along the way, we've learned what frogs and toads eat, where they live, and how they manage to avoid becoming someone else's dinner.

Now that you know so much about these fascinating creatures, you might see them differently. Maybe the next time you hear a frog's croak or a toad's trill, you'll think about all the fantastic facts you learned in this book. And perhaps you'll want to keep learning more about frogs, toads, and the incredible world of amphibians.

Thank you for joining us on this frog-tastic journey! Whether you spot a bullfrog near a pond, a tree frog clinging to a leaf, or a tiny toad in your backyard,

remember that these creatures are fun to watch and play an essential role in keeping nature in balance.

So, here's to all the fantastic frogs and terrific toads that share this world with us. And here's to you, young explorer! May your curiosity always leap as high as a frog chasing a fly!

ALL THINGS FROGS & TOADS FOR KIDS

THANK YOU!

Thank you for reading this book and for allowing us to share our love for frogs and toads with you!

If you've enjoyed this book, please let us know by leaving a rating and a brief review wherever you made your purchase! This helps us spread the word to other readers!

Thank you for your time, and have an awesome day!

For more information, please visit:
www.animalreads.com

WHAT DO FROGS DO WITH PAPER?

"Rip it! Rip it!"

© Copyright 2025 — All rights reserved Admore Publishing

ISBN: 978-3-96772-185-0

ISBN: 978-3-96772-186-7

ISBN: 978-3-96772-187-4

Animal Reads at www.animalreads.com

The content contained within this book may not be reproduced, duplicated or transmitted without direct written permission from the author or the publisher.

Under no circumstances will any blame or legal responsibility be held against the publisher, or author, for any damages, reparation, or monetary loss due to the information contained within this book. Either directly or indirectly.

Published by Admore Publishing: Gotenstraße, Berlin, Germany

www.admorepublishing.com

Made in the USA
Monee, IL
03 May 2026

49423237R00056